Rooster and Friends Go to School!

Author: Riga MD
Editor: KD Storm
Illustrator: Mr. LuQman

The story starts with Rooster on a mission to ensure everyone wakes up and catches the school bus on time.

On a foggy, rainy, yet beautiful day,
In slumber deep, the animals lay.
Rooster felt clear skies on the way;
They must catch the school bus without delay.

I am Rooster, and at dawn I raise my voice high,
Welcoming the day as we say goodbye to the night sky.
I begin the day with a joyful song,
Spreading the morning cheer all day long.

Wake up, Frog," said Rooster, eyeing the clock.
"Good morning, friend, I'm ready," said Frog.
In excitement, she leaped from rock to rock.
"I love to attend school, rain or fog."

Rooster hurries to check on the little Pup.
"How are you, dear Pup?" he asks, looking up.
"I am cool and prepared," Pup swiftly replies,
"But sunshine brings more joy to my eyes."

In dawn's embrace, Rooster calls.
To rouse Turtle, he stands tall.
Slowly, Turtle swims out of the puddle.
He says, "I know there's no more time to cuddle."

Rooster's off to motivate Duck.
"Wake up, Duck," with a peck he struck.
"Hello," said the snoozy, sleepy Duck.
She started walking, shouting, "Quack, quack!"

To wake Bunny, Rooster makes his way,
To where Bunny waits at the break of day.
"It's school time," says Rooster, "Are you set?"
And Bunny, with a smile, replies, "You bet!"

Rooster inspired Monkey, announcing the new day.
Monkey smiled and said, "I am ready to learn and play!"
Together, they took off with hand and wing,
Exploring the wonders that school would bring.

Rooster crowed, "Wake up, dear Kitty!
The sun is up, the sky is blue and pretty."
"I am ready for school," said Kitty with pride.
With joy and excitement, they walked side by side.

Rooster calls, "Rise and shine, Parrot, the morning is here!
The sun is bright, the sky is clear."
Parrot replies, "Let's head to school and start the day."
Together they learn and laugh along the way.

Rooster walks with a grin on his beak,
Awakening the Chick with a gentle tweak.
Chick flapped her wings with a smile so bright,
She shouted, "We will learn and play from morning to night!"

Excited for school, Rooster, Frog, Pup, Duck, Turtle, Bunny, Monkey, Kitty, Parrot, and Chick all hop on the bus together. Along the journey, they sing and play, chanting, "Off to school, where teachers are awesome and cool!"

SCHOOL BUS